# The Slightly Skewed
# Computer
# Dictionary

**Other Humor Books from becker&mayer!**

Bill and Al's Excellent Adventure
The Supreme Court: A Paper Doll Book
The Official Book of Thumb Wrestling
The 77 Habits of Highly Ineffective People
Golf Dirty Tricks
Armchair Golf
The J-Factor Male Jerk Counter

**Other Humor Books from Prima Publishing**

101 Uses for the Royal Family
Cat High: The Yearbook, 3rd Edition
The Artful Cat
Kids Are Still Saying the Darndest Things

**How to Order:** For information on quantity discounts contact the publisher: Prima Publishing, P.O. Box 1260BK, Rocklin, CA 95677-1260; (916) 632-4400. On your letterhead include information concerning the intended use of the books and the number of books you wish to purchase.

# The Slightly Skewed

# Computer Dictionary

## A New Angle on Computerspeak

by Doug Mayer

Drawings by John Overmyer

PRIMA

Prima Publishing
P.O. Box 1260
Rocklin, CA 95677-1260

Produced by becker&mayer!
Cover and interior design: Barrie Maguire
Electronic production: Dona McAdam, Mac on the Hill
Additional humor: Jim Becker, Claire Dederer, Stefan Grünwedel, Emily Hall, Andy Mayer, Roger Stewart, Peter Weverka

Prima Publishing and the author have attempted throughout this book to distinguish proprietary trademarks from descriptive terms by following the capitalization style used by the manufacturer. Just wanted you to know.

Information contained in this book has been obtained by Prima Publishing from sources believed to be totally unreliable. Moreover, because of the possibility of human or mechanical error by our sources, Prima Publishing, or others, the Publisher does not guarantee the accuracy, adequacy, or completeness of any information and is not responsible for any errors or omissions or the results obtained from use of such information. So there.

Library of Congress Cataloging-in-Publication Data

Mayer, Doug.
   The slightly skewed computer dictionary/Doug Mayer.
        p.        cm.
   ISBN: 1-55958-432-7 : $8.95
   1. Computers—Dictionaries.   I. Title.
QA76.15.M385   1994
004'.0207—dc20
                                                   94-19285
                                                      CIP

Printed in the United States of America
94 95 96 97 BC 10 9 8 7 6 5 4 3 2 1

For Guy and Laura.
—D.M.

For Traci, who patiently explained to me what all these words mean.
—J.O.

Special thanks to Patty Breitman.

**abort**

***abort:*** To employ a set of keystrokes to stop a traumatic computer catastrophe. Aborting can sometimes be accomplished by pressing Ctrl-C about a thousand times within five nanoseconds.

***accelerator board:*** A hardware option that enables the user to avoid buying a new computer for a period of, roughly, three to six months.

***active window:*** 1. A computer game or personal letter placed atop a series of other work files that appear to repeat infinitely into the screen's distant horizon. 2. The on-screen window available for use, but never the window needed at that particular moment.

***alias:*** An alternate name adopted by a computer-hardware purchaser who has maxed out his or her credit card.

***Alt:*** A key on IBM-style keyboards used in conjunction with other keys to execute functions such as cut, paste, delete, and save. Different software developers randomly assign different uses to each function key, such that the cranial dexterity of the user is pushed way past his or her limit.

***analog:*** A way of representing data as continuous values instead of the 1's and 0's that make up a computer's digital system. People think in analog, and computers think digitally. This single fact explains why you sometimes feel like driving a steamroller back and forth over your computer.

**Apple:** 1. A colorful and cute logo that, when placed on a computer, makes the computer entirely irresistible to shoppers. 2. The name of the world's largest secular cult.

**AppleTalk:** 1. A rapidly evolving vocabulary relating only to the most current products. 2. What apples say to one another in private.

**application:** 1. A form used to file for job openings or places in private schools and colleges. Applications are often rejected, resulting in rejection parties and, much later in life, a low sense of self-worth (see *psychotherapy* and *Dangerfield Syndrome*). 2. A computer program with much the same properties.

**architecture:** 1. The internal arrangement of integrated circuits in a computer, meticulously designed by a computer architect whose work is only ever seen by over-worked technicians. Unlike architects who design houses, computer architects always seem to design computers that can never be expanded or otherwise added onto.

**archive:** A dusty, little-visited section of a computer system where one stores the files that one desperately hopes one will never have to see again.

**artificial intelligence:** The goal of many computer scientists, artificial intelligence is a computer's ability to mimic human thought processes, thereby making the computer moody, irrational, and prone to show up late on Mondays.

## *artificial intelligence*

**bar codes**

**ASCII files:** A basic format understood by all computers, ASCII stands for "Any Stupid Computer Interprets It," or "Any Smart Computer Interprets It," depending on what kind of day you're having.

**auto dial:** A system that "automatically" dials a phone number for you—after you first enter the phone number into memory, enter the correct command to dial the selected number, and then hold up the phone to the computer's speaker. The rest is automatic.

**b**ackground printing: 1. A technique designed to help users forget that they have recently printed a document.
2. A means by which an already-slow computer printer can be made to print at an even slower rate.

**backing up:** The making and saving of duplicate files that begins immediately following a hard disk crash.

**balloon help:** 1. A highly advanced new system technology that creates tiny, cartoon-like balloons that provide just enough information to further bewilder the user.

**bar codes:** 1. Yet another obtuse language that only computers can read. 2. Rules of behavior and good conduct in a drinking establishment, such as, don't use "What's your sign?" as a pick-up line and be sure to leave a tip.

***batch file:*** A computer file designed to accept batches of toll house cookies as bribes, in exchange for which any command you use on the file might work.

***baud:*** A measure of data transmission speed. Data transmission systems (devised in secret by long-distance telephone carriers and computer manufacturers) were designed to send computer data at one of several very slow speeds, resulting in a significant and otherwise unobtainable income boost for the carriers. A percentage of these extravagant profits is funneled back to the computer manufacturer as a way of saying "thanks!"

***BBS:*** An electronic meeting place in which people, via their computers and phone lines, post bulletins and swap BS (see *electronically swinging singles*).

***bit:*** 1. A very little piece of information, as in "I wrote a document on my word-processing program, but so far I've finished only a very little bit." 2. The past tense of byte.

***bitmap:*** An itty-bitty map.

***boot:*** To kick or otherwise manually send a computer into flight.

**bug**

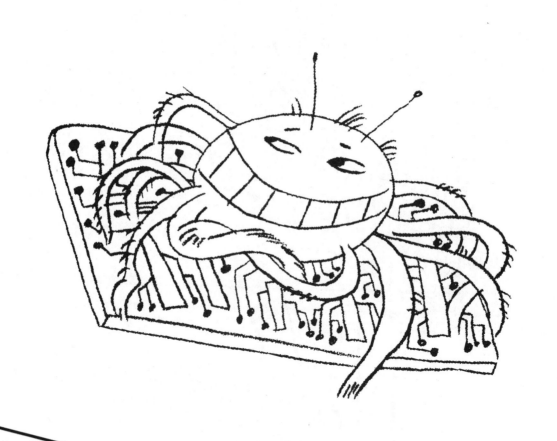

**boot disk:** 1. All the instructions your computer needs to start up in the morning, though it does not include a cup of coffee. The crucial quality of the boot disk makes it almost impossible to find when you need it. 2. A disk you can kick or otherwise manually send into flight if you're afraid of breaking your foot by booting your computer.

**buffer:** 1. An apprentice at a computer repair department whose job it is to shine and wax computers, giving them the appearance that they have been thoroughly repaired. 2. Anyone who throws his or her body between you and the computer you're running at with a hacksaw.

**bug:** 1. A small insect that often nests on computer hard drives or power supplies. 2. A means by which at least one hundred hours of data entry can be completely and irrevocably destroyed in a single keystroke (see *undocumented feature*).

**bus:** A main circuit used to send computer data. Advanced computers use high-speed buses, which sometimes roll over data embankments and explode, just like in the movies.

**byte:** 1. A piece of information or storage space so small it is often referred to as the Italian lira of data. One million bytes equals one megabyte, which is still not much space but will buy the user a little time while more space is found. 2. Bad or awful, as in "This new piece of hardware really bytes."

***Cache:*** A reserved section of memory, so named because it is hidden in the computer and is difficult to locate. Pronounced "cash," as in "I need more cash for a bigger cache."

***CAD:*** Acronym for "Computer Aided Design." An engineering function for computers in which enormously expensive computers are used to replicate the work of high-school level drafting students.

***CD-ROM:*** The cutting edge of technology, which allows people to store and use more information than ever before. CD-ROMs are extremely useful if you've always wanted a catalog of all your shopping lists back to 1972, a detailed list of Imelda Marcos's shoe collection, or an international inventory of Charles and Di articles (from both American and British tabloids). A user can sometimes play music from a compact disc in a CD-ROM drive. Most computers, unfortunately, show a marked preference for Englebert Humperdink.

***chaos:*** The normal state of affairs when one is trying to make sense of a computer's actions. Chaos occurs because people tend to be logical and dependable, while computers tend to be moody, unreliable, and unfathomably irrational. Chaos should not be confused with KAOS, the enemy spy agency in "Get Smart."

**character:** There are 128 characters currently used for exchanging information between users and computers. This is good for most computer users, but an unfortunate situation for Tibetans, who have over 20,000 characters in their language, thereby making their keyboards approximately the size of a Wal-Mart store.

**character recognition:** A computer's ability to sense the personality of its user and respond accordingly.

**chip:** A section or piece of a laptop that has been dropped while in transit.

**Chooser:** The grade school child who is always selected by the teacher to pick a side for the kickball team. Some people go through childhood without ever being the chooser, which invariably leads them to a computer-related career where they believe that they are finally in control. Alas, they are not.

**circuit board:** A flat plastic board designed by manufacturers to secure integrated circuits permanently so that they may not be readily upgraded.

**click:** 1. A small, exclusive circle of computer nerds. 2. A term for the act of pressing the button on a mouse, so named because, well, it clicks.

**clip art:** 1. Artwork that has been digitally modified to appear ragged around the edges. 2. A cheap illustration that indicates that a document was created with desktop publishing (see *Mixed Doubles Luge Biweekly*).

**Clipboard:** A utility that displays text that has just been cut. Useful for users with profound short-term memory problems.

**clone:** *clone:*

**command:** An oral order given by the user to the computer. Some frequently overheard commands include, "Print, you idiot," "Oh, hurry up," and "No! Stop! Don't do that!"

**Command key:** A bonus key on Apple keyboards imprinted with a cute Apple logo. Rarely used, the Command key is strategically placed so that it is easy to hit accidentally.

**compatibility:** The ability of different pieces of hardware and software to function together smoothly and reliably. Hardware designers have proven compatibility to be a theoretical impossibility, much like the perpetual motion machine and world peace.

**computer:** An elaborate IBM- or Macintosh-designed habitat for your gerbil. Comes equipped with gerbil-sized treadmill to generate power.

**CONFIG.SYS:** The file that controls the DOS and OS/2 operating systems. Fooling around with this file is the pastime of a certain specialized nerd known as a "CONFIG sissy."

**consultant**

**configuration:**   What the technical support person says you've messed up, no matter what problem you're having (see *self-esteem*).

**consultant:**   Any person who charges at least $50 per hour to explain in simple English the text of a new computer manual.

**Control key:**   A key included on IBM-style keyboards— at the urging of psychiatrist Dr. Heinrich Flauberhosen—to satisfy control freaks. The Control key gives users the illusion of control over their computers and, by extension, their egos, superegos, and ids.

**converter:**   A religious zealot who rings a user's doorbell at the exact moment necessary to cause the user to somehow wreak havoc on a file.

**copy protection:**   A built-in feature on computer software designed so that only your devious local hacker can copy the program.

**CPU:**   In IBM PC-compatible computers, the chip that is named by a five-digit number, the last two of which are 86 for no apparent reason. Macs, in a typical nose-thumbing gesture, use a five-digit number that begins with 68. Go figure.

**crash:** The complete and irrevocable destruction of a computer's hard disk, often caused by something large and dangerous such as a cat hair or smoke particle, or by the computer's own ornery character. Following a hard disk crash, the victim (the "crash dummy") begins a new and short-lived phase known as "disk backup."

**cursor:** 1. Anyone who has spent more than ten minutes with a computer. The cursor inflicts curses, some of which include, "Out, ye viral plague," "Damn thee to a fiery eternity, O slow machine," and "Curs'd art thou, mangy pox-ridden printer." 2. A blinking vertical bar in the text that shows the cursor where to direct his or her curse.

**custom software:** Software designed by a computer consultant for you to use on your computer. Custom software is then sold to many other users, often resulting in enormous profits for the consultant who designed the program at your expense.

**cut:** To slice a paragraph, body part, or piece of computer hardware with a sharp instrument such as a knife or disk fragment.

**cut and paste:** A "simple" technique used to move text from one location to another. The user moves the cursor over to the beginning of the section to be cut, clicks, selects the section, selects "Cut" from a menu, moves the cursor to the new location, finds that same menu, selects "Paste" and—simple as

## daisy-wheel printer

that—*voilà*, the text is in its new location, which not infrequently is the wrong location. This function makes you wonder if we've progressed at all from the days of safety scissors and edible paste.

**cyberpunk:** The same old computer nerd in brand-new leather pants. Not to be confused with cyberdisco or cybercountry-and-western.

**daisy chain:** A way of connecting computer hardware in sequence such that a failure in one unit will cause everything after it to catch fire, blow up, or release smoke.

**daisy-wheel printer:** An ancient form of printing dating all the way back to the early Greek and Roman empires. The earliest daisy-wheel printers consisted of an enormous stone tablet, over one hundred tons in weight, to which 26 thieves were affixed in sequence, each holding an 18-pound, three-feet-high carving of a letter and a large rubber stamp pad. Some stubborn counterculturists insist on using a slight modification of this printer even to this day.

**data:** 1. Information stored in a computer. Data should not be confused with Dada, the artistic movement based upon irrationality and the destruction of conventional artistic norms. 2. Name of goofy-looking character from "Star Trek: The Next Generation."

**database:** A computer application that sorts and stores unfathomable amounts of information such that movie freaks with their own databases can tell you how many times the line "I'm having an old friend for dinner" or "I love the smell of napalm in the morning" have been spoken.

**data compression:** A program that functions as the trash compactor of the computer world, efficiently squeezing data so that it fits into a tiny space, every now and then mangling everything in the process.

**data decompression:** The reverse of data compression, the digital equivalent of taking the garbage out of the compactor and trying frantically to make sense of it all again.

**data flow:** Data flow is controlled by data spigots, data flow valves, and data flush levers. A lot of data on a small wire or cable can result in a data overflow or data backup, which may require the services of a data plumber.

**data processors:** What typists now call themselves (see *overeducated twentysomething slackers*).

**debugger:** Bronx computer terminology for "computer," as in "De bugger don't woirk. It's gots some kinda problem."

**default:** Bronx computer terminology indicating blame, as in "I knows how come it don't woirk. It's de fault a friggin' IBM."

**debugger**

**dialog box**

**delete:** One of the very few commands that, when entered, is final. Once a file is deleted, no amount of sobbing, clicking of heels, praying, or promising to be a better person in the future will bring it back.

**density:** 1. The relative thickness of the skull surrounding a user's cranial cavity. 2. The relative amount of information that can be stored and completely lost or irretrievably damaged on one computer disk.

**desk accessory:** A vase, photo, or small memento.

**desktop:** The visual display of the computer screen located on the front surface of the computer, which usually sits atop the real desktop.

**desktop publishing:** Word-processing and formatting programs that enable all would-be publishers to produce their own magazines, newspapers, or books. This has led to a great number of diverse new publications, including *The M.A.P.H. (Mothers Against Preteen Hackers) Digest* and *The Bill and Barbara Weekly: A Look at What We Did Last Week.*

**dialog box:** An on-screen box that enables the user to have a dialog with the computer in much the same way that a terrorist conducts a dialog with a hostage. The user is allowed only one response, which is almost always "Okay."

**digital:** 1. A computer's system of using 1's and 0's to obscure its true personality, which is invariably stubborn and irrational. This system is used because computers are too stupid to count past the number one. 2. A system that makes musical recordings sound just a little bit better so that they can be sold for a whole lot more. 3. A marketing term used to assist a purchaser in rationalizing the expenditure of a large sum of money.

**digitize:** To add ragged or jagged edges to a photo or drawing.

**dingbats:** 1. A computer font that is the word-processing equivalent of speaking in tongues. Useful for writing bomb threats. 2. Used in the singular, an affectionate form of address among computer techies.

**DIP switch:** An ultraminiature set of switches soldered to a printed circuit board. So named because only a real dip would attempt to switch the settings.

**directory:** A DOS listing of files on a screen that doesn't really give the user a sense of where he or she really is. Computer directories were designed with the saying "Wherever you go, there you are" in mind.

**dot-matrix printer**

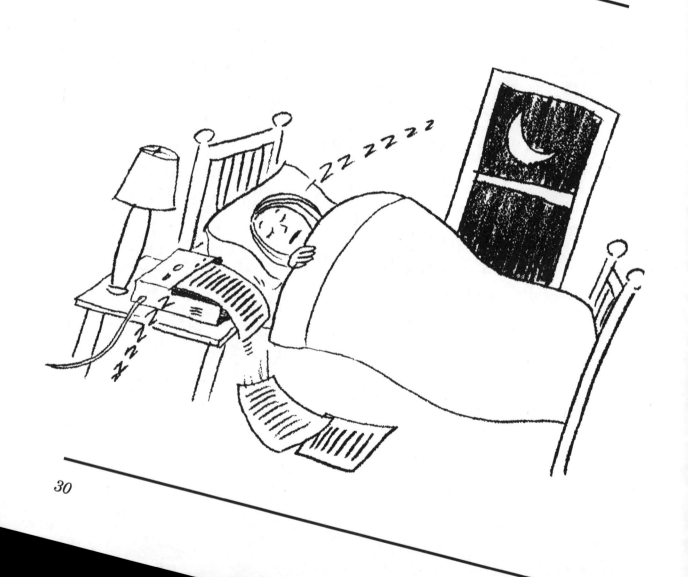

**diskette:** 1. A small, portable disk that can be readily transported anywhere. However, the data on a diskette can be instantly destroyed by such uncommon things as sunlight, magnetic fields, liquids, high temperatures, low temperatures, and sharp objects such as pencils, pens, and paper clips. 2. An MIT cheerleader.

**display:** A small television that has been installed on the front surface of the computer. The display receives only one channel, which never has any good shows on it.

**document:** A word-processing file. The word is derived from the Greek *doci* (hidden) and *mentum* (never to return).

**dot-matrix printer:** 1. A printer on which hundreds of tiny dots (which appear to the eye as ten or twelve large dots) are used to create text. 2. A printer that requires roughly an entire working day to print a five page document. 3. The reason laser printers exist.

**double-click:** Click. Click.

**double-density:** 1. A means of risking the loss or destruction of twice the amount of data on a computer disk at three to four times the cost of a normal disk. 2. An especially slow-witted user. 3. The consistency of the cheese on your pizza after a week—or of your posterior after a year of spreadsheets, word processing, and Tetris.

**download:** The act of sending mucho dinero from one's bank account to that of a computer manufacturer or software supplier.

**downtime:** 1. An all-out, no-holds-barred failure of a computer or computer network, which rarely occurs outside of the 24- to 48-hour period immediately prior to a major deadline. 2. A reminder from an under-appreciated computer that it must never, ever be taken for granted.

**dpi:** 1. A measure of the number of dots per inch that any given printer can print. Currently a matter of speculation, since no one has ever bothered to count. 2. An acronym for Microsoft's late-night software development team, the "Department of Prolific Insomniacs".

**drag and drop:** 1. The accidental placement of a file deep into a series of folders such that it will, in all likelihood, never be found again. 2. How people moved their computers around before the invention of the laptop.

**drive:** (Derived from the verb "drive," as in "This stupid machine is driving me up the wall and down the other side.") A device that accepts a highly sensitive magnetic disk, opens its protective metal slide cover, and spins the disk at an extremely high speed while simultaneously dragging it over a gunk-encrusted head. The drive also accepts pliers, tweezers, paper clips, pens, and pencils,

**downtime**

**echo**

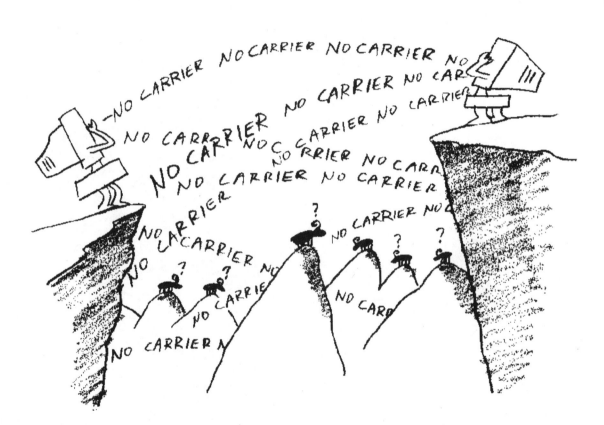

which is good, since all of these tools are needed if you ever want to see your disk again.

**dump:** A colloquial term describing what happens when a computer user's girlfriend or boyfriend terminates the connection for reasons of incompatability or some other bug in the program. Often accompanied by the pitching of certain desk accessories off one's desk.

***e**cho:* A A communications communications standard standard, , such such that that the the data data sent sent by by a a computer computer is is sent sent back back by the the receiving receiving computer computer, , giving giving the the user user the the impression impression that that he he or or she she is is doing doing everything everything twice twice. .

**edit:** To make (usually) unwanted or (generally) undesired changes to a document. Editing is usually done in three steps. First, an unwanted edit is made accidentally. Second, another change is made to correct the first. Finally, the user realizes that the first change should not have been made, recognizes that it is already too late to use the "Undo" function, and heads to the nearest watering hole for a stiff drink.

**eject:** The button on an F-16 (or similar aircraft) that is depressed immediately after the on-board computer has crashed.

**e-mail:** 1. A computer-based system used to communicate with friends and relatives. E-mail is popular at work, since users can send jokes, "Star Trek" trivia, and long love letters—all while appearing to be working diligently at their terminals. E-mail provides a forum for surreptitiously quizzing your co-workers about their late-night activities, car mileage, toilet paper preferences, and other vital issues. 2. The only known way to communicate with Bill Gates, who is suspected to exist only as a hologram at the e-mail address "billg @microsoft.com."

**environment:** That which is being rapidly depleted by microchip-producing factories all over the country.

**error message:** Panic-inducing hijinks on the computer's part. It's called an "error message" because it makes the mistake of telling the user that something's wrong without dropping a clue about how to fix it.

**Escape:** The button on IBM-style keyboards abbreviated Esc, which is really short for "Escuse me! I take it back! I really, really didn't want to do that! Please stop it now!"

**expansion slot:** An internal computer design. It's called an "expansion slot" because it expands to accept the increasing amount of money you stuff into your computer to keep it happy.

## *expansion slot*

**file**

***extended warranty:***  Additional warranty period which, if purchased, virtually guarantees that your computer will not require its use. Conversely, if the extended warranty is not purchased, your computer will almost certainly explode minutes after the standard warranty expires (see *Jean-Paul Sartre's* No Exit).

***f** ax:*  From the word "facsimile," meaning "like the original, only a whole lot blurrier and harder to read."

***fax/modem:***  A confused piece of hardware that functions as a modem when it's supposed to be a fax machine and works as a fax when you need a modem. Some fax/modems are equipped with a speaker so you can listen to the voices of important clients cursing when they accidentally receive fax tones.

***fax switch:***  An electronic device meant to route fax calls to the computer and voice calls to the telephone. Ironically, no manufacturer has developed a fax switch that works properly, and in actual use the routing of the call is randomly determined.

***file:***  A text document or other collection of data. There are five different types of files—missing, lost, damaged, destroyed, and those that have not yet had one of these things happen to them, but are about to.

**file server:** The central storage and processing computer, which concentrates information and processing tasks so that all computers fail simultaneously, thus leading to ad hoc office parties and afternoons off.

**Finder:** An ironic term coined by Apple programmers noted for their dry sense of humor. The term "Finder" is somewhat akin to a three-legged dog named "Lucky."

**floppy disk:** A disk encased in hard, rigid plastic.

**folder:** A Macintosh screen icon whose function is to accept a file for storage, thereby keeping the file hidden from convenient view. Folders can be placed inside of other folders ad infinitum, creating a multi-tier system. This format gives the screen a fascinating Escher-like appearance when many layers of folders are open, which is interesting but not too helpful.

**font:** Sets of type characters that are available for use on a computer. Some people are font monogamists, choosing a font and standing by it loyally. Others are font sluts, hoping that with each new typeface they won't make the same old grammatical mistakes.

**footer:** Common text or blank lines at the bottom of each page of a printed document, generally used to carefully pad a term paper such that an assigned page length is achieved without requiring additional work.

*footprint*

**footprint:** Amount of desk space required by a computer. This does not, of course, include room for the mouse, mouse pad, wiring, disks, or common items such as a modem, printer, external disk drive, tape backup, CD-ROM, manuals, etc. For these the user may require an additional desk or two.

**format:** 1. To initialize a new disk. During the initialization, the computer divides the disk into several internal sectors, including "storage," "vast waste-land," "lost and found," and "never-never land." 2. The layout of text in a word-processing document such that the setting of indentations, spacings, font sizes and styles, page orientations, and page widths and lengths all combine to create a task that takes almost as much time as the writing of the text.

**freeware and shareware:** Software that can be used at no or very low cost. Developed by aging hippies as a poor substitute for free love. Of course, you may still get a virus.

**function:** A programming term that is too advanced to be defined in *The Slightly Skewed Computer Dictionary*. Its use in everyday language, however, is a certain sign that one is in the presence of a genuine nerd (see *the face in your bathroom mirror*).

**glitch:** Source of the age-old computer nerd motto, "Life's a glitch, and then you die."

**graphics:**   The capability of a computer to simulate arcade-quality video games, such as Mortal Combat and Sonic the Hedgehog. No quarters need to be deposited, though thousands of dollars may be required to purchase the high-resolution color monitor.

***h**acker:*   A computer nerd turned ugly. Hackers spend countless late-night hours with their computers, modems, and phone lines gaining access to unimportant data such as the CIA double agent database, AT&T's calling-card numbers, and Kazakhstan nuclear missile codes (see *twelve-year-olds who shame you with their knowledge and can access your credit card*).

**handshake:**   1. A hand shake. 2. A signal sent between computers to establish an electronic link. Computers have varying styles of handshakes. IBM uses a firm handshake with a backslap protocol, while Apple prefers a high-five, thumbs-up system protocol.

**hard copy:**   A printed copy of a given document, which can be eaten by the user's dog rather than lost in a hard-disk crash.

**hardware:**   The variety of off-white, beige, and tan boxes of assorted dimensions that make up a computer system. Hardware is so named because it is often hard to figure out where to connect it.

## handshake

## *head crash*

**head crash:** When a computer user's head strikes the monitor or the desktop, usually resulting in a dull "thud" sound, much like the sound of wood or rocks colliding. In extreme cases, the head may become imbedded in the monitor, requiring both units to be returned to the factory.

**help:** 1. An on-line tool containing most everything you need to know to get through a day with your computer. This is a convenient feature for those users who are incapable of reaching for and opening a book. 2. A Beatles movie not yet available on CD-ROM.

**highlight:** A technique by which whole paragraphs or pages can be selected so that they may be accidentally destroyed or irrevocably altered in a single keystroke.

**high resolution:** A quality of graphic resolution such that the image appears not as a series of gigantic dots with ragged edges, but rather as a compilation of countless smaller dots, with only slightly less ragged edges.

**home:** Mantra favored by office workers wishing to return to the beginning of a document. The word "home" is said serenely in the "click" position (spine straight, legs uncrossed, hand on mouse, breathing in through the left nostril and out through the right) and is repeated until all vile thoughts and vibes poisonous to your computer have left your mind.

47

***I**BM:* Three letters once used to designate what was once the predominant personal-computer manufacturer and what is now a verb frequently used on Wall Street in sentences such as "My life savings just got IBMed in the stock market! Where's the window?"

*icon:* A screen illustration representing a software program or document. The word is a contraction of the phrase "I con't read," the oft-repeated phrase of British computer neophytes. Icons are useful for users who didn't touch a computer until they were twenty-five or older—and thus have the computer savvy of four-year-olds.

*import:* The act of bringing a file into a new word-processing program. In the process, such insignificant items as formatting, fonts, font styles, and layouts are left behind at the border.

*information superhighway:* 1. A bumpy road with bad signage and expensive tolls that is still under construction. 2. The world's most overworked metaphor.

*insert:* A word-processing technique that places new text in between previously created text. For example, the sentence "Computers are our *friends*!" could be altered to read "Computers are hellish, nightmarish machines to which we have become enslaved. They could hardly be considered our *friends*!"

## *information superhighway*

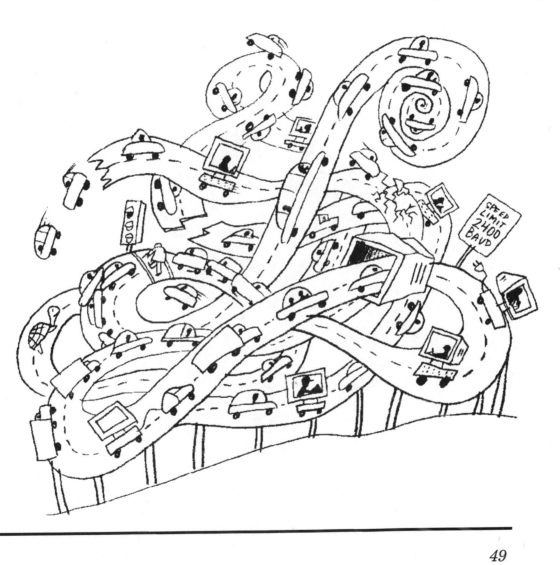

*interface*

**install:** 1. The placement of a program on a hard disk, at which time viruses, dust particles, and a random assortment of dirt and debris are also installed. 2. Same as "installment," which is the only feasible way to purchase that new computer that you probably don't need and definitely can't afford, but really, really want to have a whole lot.

**interactive video:** Digital video where you get to make choices from a menu concerning what happens next. For example, you could have Scarlet O'Hara and Rhett Butler kiss and make up, or turn Hannibal Lecter into a vegetarian.

**interface:** 1. The point of interaction between a computer and its user, and often the cause of such computer-induced maneuvers as the CRT head butt, the keyboard fist slam, and the around-the-world mouse launch. In extreme cases, hardware accessories such as sledgehammers, circular saws, and dynamite may be used to interface with a computer. 2. Two computer nerds on a date.

**Internet:** A worldwide interconnected computer network of university and research facilities designed to facilitate the rapid exchange of information. Internet is used primarily by college students to set up blind dates, trade jokes, and generally kill time between classes.

***i/o:*** 1. Short for "input/output." 2. Also short for "it's/ over," the situation users find themselves in after accidentally reversing "inputs" and "outputs" and applying power.

***J**aggies:* The complete and utter inability of any computer to draw a simple diagonal line. Jaggies, a perfectly geometric staircase looking nothing like a diagonal line at all, are found in even the most advanced graphics packages (see *crinkle-cut fries*).

***joystick:*** 1. An input control lever encased in a very thin and fragile plastic case. Used frequently in computer games where the user commonly gets flustered and, in a surge of adrenaline, accidentally rips the lever from the plastic enclosure. 2. A slang term whose definition a reputable publisher would never, ever allow in a wholesome, family-oriented book such as this.

***justify:*** Refers to rationalization techniques used to explain to yourself and others why you would rather spend the weekend installing an electronic Rolodex on your hard disk than simply get a real Rolodex, or a real life.

***K**:* Abbreviation of the user exclamation "K-blooey," which frequently occurs after a program crashes due to insufficient memory.

*justify*

**laptop**

**keyboard:**   A detachable unit of keys used for entering the letters of the alphabet into a computer. Since there are only 26 letters in the alphabet, and keyboards are designed with lots of extra keys, manufacturers include such symbols as @{}<>~ (')#^*. Unfortunately, these are useful only if you happen to be a foul-mouthed cartoon character.

**keypad:**   A bonus appendage to a keyboard containing the numbers 0 through 9, only in a different pattern. The keypad is never used unless the user has previous experience as a supermarket checkout clerk.

**laptop:**   A computer that might fit in your lap if you were Arnold Schwarzenegger. For most of us, a laptop requires a couple of additional laps.

**laser printer:**   A computer printer that eliminates the incessant whine of a dot-matrix printer, but only at great cost. Despite its name, a laser has yet to be found in one of these printers.

**letter quality:**   Any printer whose type does not resemble tiny Lego building blocks.

**local bus:**   An expansion slot that is connected directly to a PC's microprocessor and therefore runs very quickly. This should not be confused with your local neighborhood bus, which operates inordinately slowly, due to the minimal computing power of the unit's CPU, which is usually named Ralph or Vinny.

**m**achine language: For years, the world's most highly trained anthropologists and linguists have sought the source of the machine language. Some believe it can be traced back to an ancient tablet found in Palus Altus, which is inscribed with a mysterious dot-dash code that no one has been able to crack. A computer in South America, when programmed with this code, began to spew out recipes for guacamole quiche. Another school of anthropologists asserts that the tablet was just a place to wipe your sandals.

*macro:* Short for the French phrase *Ma croix est la fou de la merde*, which roughly translates "I'm really tired of repeating these stupid little tasks over and over again. Can't we automate them?"

*mail merge:* A means of merging names and addresses with a form letter such that enormous, faceless mail-order houses can sound like old college chums.

*mainframe:* In order to qualify as a mainframe, a computer must be able to house approximately 1,200 gerbils (and their treadmills).

*megabyte:* A measure of information storage capacity equal to one million bytes, which sounds like a lot but is not really enough space to store much of anything.

## *mail merge*

**menu**

**megahertz:**   1. Latin word meaning "many, many hertz."
2. The speed at which a computer operates,
which is usually about three gizillion times
faster than the user operates.

**memory:**   Data-storage device for a computer or a human
brain. In either case, there is never enough, it
often works improperly or fails outright, and it
is very hard to fix when broken.

**menu:**   A set of choices on a computer screen, none of
which will be even vaguely appealing (see *Vern
& Carla's Weenie Barn*).

**microprocessor chip:**   The single most important integrated circuit in
a computer which, though it never, ever breaks,
still needs to be replaced every year. By sheer
coincidence, the only means of replacing a microprocessor chip is by purchasing a new computer.

**Microsoft:**   Software manufacturing company of such extra-
ordinarily huge size and enormous wealth that
it seems to be some kind of illegal monopoly,
but isn't.

**modem:**   1. An accessory with a number of LEDs that
flash and blink at seemingly random intervals,
indicating that the unit is apparently working
properly. 2. The interface between the computer
and telephone line, so that computer viruses may
be received without the time-consuming exchange
of disks.

***monitor:*** The screen at the front of the computer which is the cause of a well-documented disorder called "monitor envy." No matter the size of their monitors, almost all users suffer from this malady. Graphic designers, with their sports-bar-television-sized screens, cruelly lord it over students, accountants, and librarians, whose monitors usually resemble little gray handkerchiefs.

***motherboard:*** The central circuit board in a computer, the motherboard is home to the CPU, expansion slots, ROM, and RAM. In a dysfunctional computer, the motherboard is often to blame for the erratic behavior of the childrenboard.

***mouse:*** A distinctly un-rodent-like piece of hardware that is neither fuzzy nor cute. Like a mouse, however, it has its own agenda and is quite unlikely to give a damn about what you want it to do.

***multimedia:*** Involving more than one medium, such as graphics, video, or sound. The use of multimedia software is inherently more fun than regular computing, since it is more like watching MTV (see *generation of adults with limited attention spans*).

***nanosecond:*** The split-second during which a user's brain realizes that it is about to press the wrong button—and also realizes that it is too late to stop that action.

*network*

**nerd:**    Any person who reads a humorous book of computer definitions in his or her free time.

**network:**    That unfathomable pile of wires in the middle of the office. If all the cables used for networking were connected end to end, they would reach all the way from earth to the planet Vulcan.

**nibble:**    Half a byte, equal to four bits. A nibble should not be confused with a munch (three bits), a chomp (nine bits), a gulp (a munch and a chomp) or an Oprah (five munches, a gulp, and a few sips of coffee).

**notebook:**    A small computer that simulates the features associated with a notebook, pencil, and eraser, but costs thousands of dollars and operates for less than three hours before needing recharging.

**Old-timer:**    Any person who has seen or knows how to operate the interface on an unpowered typewriter. The typewriter was a desktop ASCII character-printing device used during the Paleozoic era.

**online service:**    The computer equivalent of a 1-900 number, though preying on an altogether different set of compulsions.

**OOP:** 1. Acronym for "object-oriented" programming, a new way of designing software without having to know any programming language whatsoever, guaranteed. 2. One of the new designer fragrances that competes with Hanel, Bsession, and Pium.

**operating system:** The program that actually runs your computer, connecting your hardware to the software you are using. An operating system is the computer middle-man of the software world, because it costs a lot of money, it causes hassles, and no one is really sure just what sort of useful purpose it serves.

**page break:** A demarcation between pages. When writing letters with a word-processing program, the page break almost always occurs after the word "Sincerely" and immediately before the letter writer's name.

**palmtop:** A miniature computer, such as Apple's Newton, that is sized to fit in the palm of an NBA superstar over seven feet tall. He can't, however, spin it on his finger.

**parallel port:** 1. A plug on the back of your computer that supposedly sends data much faster than a serial port, but looks suspiciously similar. 2. A means of connecting peripherals to a computer. The manufacturer calculates the needed number of ports on each computer, then subtracts three during the manufacturing process.

**palmtop**

**password**

**parity:** A means of guaranteeing complete accuracy when transmitting or receiving data, parity makes sure that the computer user receives text such as "Regarding your test results zergsplotchj* (^@gurgle^%#$()#{})_*! ARrrghh you that...."

**park:** A means of securing the head on a disk drive. If the head isn't parked, it could drive around, crashing, leaving skid marks, and generally burning some hard-disk rubber wherever it so pleases—which usually means on the folder or directory you just created called "Really Important Stuff."

**password:** Any word in any language that is difficult to remember when one is under stress (see *a computer user's first or last name*).

**PC:** Useful acronym for the phrases "personal computer," "professional consultant," "politically correct," and "permanently cooked," as in, "I hired a PC PC to network my PCs. As it turns out, he wasn't that good a PC and now all my PCs are PC."

**PCMCIA:** 1. The slots in laptops and fax/modems for pulse code modulation. 2. A long, unfathomable Roman numeral.

**PDA:** Acronym for the phrases "personal digital assistant" or "pay more dollars to Apple."

67

**pie chart:** 1. Graphic representation of data in a pie-shaped chart. Some commonly used pie charts include the Mom's Apple Pie Chart, the Bananas-and-Whipped-Cream Pie Chart, and the Pie-in-Your-Face Chart. 2. A CD-ROM chart of over 30,000 pies of the world, including Turkish Turkey Potpie and Yeti Snow Pie.

**pirate:** A computer thief who steals software by copying it. Unlike pirates of yesteryear, contemporary pirates are not very colorful, do not own scabbards, and do not say things like "Aye, walk the plank matey!" In fact, a computer pirate pretty much looks and sounds like a normal user, except he or she has that guilty "gosh, I know I shouldn't have done that" look that you sometimes see on golden retrievers.

**pixel:** A mythical computer fairy that has been known to descend upon computer users, rectifying catastrophic programming errors or hard disk crashes with a wave of her cordless mouse.

**port:** A connection into or out of a computer. At the port of entry, data that does not give the proper secret "handshake" is denied entry and is dumped overboard.

**pirate**

**product support**

**printer:**   A computer output device that places graphics and text onto paper. The first printers were guys in dirty aprons whose hands were all covered in ink and said, "That'll be ready in ten weeks." The next step out of the primordial printer soup were the (much faster) dot-matrix printers, which were about as noisy as sitting by the speakers at an Aerosmith concert. The newest printers are supposedly much quieter, but no one knows for sure because of the hearing loss from using dot-matrix printers. Besides, when you take them to the repair shop, the clean-cut guy behind the counter invariably says, "That'll be ready in ten weeks."

**product support:**   The division of a software manufacturer responsible for answering users' questions—*if* you can ever get your call through. Product support is either composed of young, untrained interns who give you flagrantly incorrect (if creative) suggestions, or sophisticated, highly trained computer programmers who provide patronizing and condescending answers you can't understand anyway.

**program:**   A scheduled time-segment of one-half or one hour, during which a particular story or plot is continued from week to week. Some examples of programs are "The Munsters," "Mork and Mindy," and "I Dream of Genie."

***q**ueue:* 1. A fancy, stuck-up British word that has nothing to do with the letter *Q* at all and actually means "waiting in line." 2. A recurring character on "Star Trek: The Next Generation."

*Quicken:* A financial software package that enables you to track your finances precisely, so that you may spend money more quickly and know precisely when you'll reach rock-bottom. Curiously, the Quicken user manual does not begin with Chapter 1, but with Chapter 11.

*quit:* Computer command that allows the user to leave the program. Programmers have named this function "Quit" rather than " 'Til Tomorrow," "Take a Break," or "Hope to See You Again Soon," because they know that you will probably be frustrated, exhausted, and pretty much at wit's end when you select it.

***r**ead-only:* A document on a disk or any other medium that can be read but cannot be written over. Some examples of read-only documents include the Declaration of Independence, control room copies of "How to Run This Nuclear Plant," and the original copy of *War and Peace*.

*relational database:* A database that shows the relationship of various family members. Useful when a guest appears at a holiday event who seems out of place or who looks like a party crasher.

**reset**

**reset:**   A hardware or software command that puts all operating settings back to their original values. However, some users opt to reset their computers by heaving them from great heights onto sidewalks (see *anger management workshop*).

**resolution:**   An oft-broken promise made by computer users, such as to back up a hard disk frequently.

**restart:**   To take it from the top, as in "Now that my computer has re-jected this re-formatted disk, I'm going to re-start it and re-try it, and if it doesn't work this time I'm going to re-load my re-volver and re-tire this re-volting machine for good" (see *advanced anger management workshop*).

**Return:**   A key on the computer keyboard whose name is derived from the ancient typewriter machine. There are soft returns, when one is being nice and gentle with one's computer, and hard returns, which are used to prove to the inanimate computer that you really, really hate it a whole lot.

**root directory:**   The first and primary directory on a DOS-formatted hard disk—the closest thing to home. If you're lost, you can find your way back by tapping your heels three times together and repeating, "There's no place like the root directory! There's no place like the root directory! There's no place like the root directory!"

***ruler:*** 1. A horizontal icon bar at the top of a word-processing document. The ruler has numbers just like a real ruler and also has lots of cute little triangles, buttons, and other things that, when clicked, forever change your document in a completely unpredictable way. 2. A computer with delusions of grandeur, as in "I am the ruler of this office!" This fantasy derives from the fact that the computer is short, bald, and fat, just like Mussolini.

***run time:*** A premonition preceding an enormous power surge that causes the user to run quickly far, far away from his or her computer.

***Salvage:*** To save a portion of a file that one's computer has targeted for destruction, making you feel a little like James Bond.

***save:*** The act of storing a computer file to disk. Seldom used except immediately following power outages or lightning strikes when it is used frequently for a short period of time.

***scanner:*** Yet another piece of show-offy graphic-design hardware through which the designer renders useless your entire day's paste-up work. In this case, the designer says "I'll just scan it" and makes the necessary changes in, yes, a nanosecond.

**ruler**

**scuzzy**

**scratchpad:** 1. The section of a computer's memory used only for temporary data storage. 2. A computer user's brain.

**screen saver:** A graphics program that prolongs the life of a screen by using $5,000 worth of computer hardware to simulate a bowl of fish or a dancing Macintosh. Often more conceptually challenging than what you're actually using the computer for.

**scroll:** A means of moving through a word-processing file, viewing one portion at a time. Now that the Dead Sea Scrolls are online, you can scroll through the Scrolls.

**scuzzy:** 1. The pronunciation of SCSI, which stands for "small computer system interface." 2. One's second-grade perception of the opposite sex.

**serial port:** The port on the rear of the computer that is closest to the machine's serial number imprint. Nearby ports include the quality control stamp port, the right-next-to-that-switch-with-the-one-and-zero port, and the FCC-sticker port.

**session:** The period of time a user is at a computer terminal or at a psychiatrist's office. The amounts of both times are usually directly related to one another.

**shut down:** An idyllic, nirvana-like state in which annoying computer glitches, warning messages, and lost files all magically cease to be, simply through the removal of power to the computer. This can occur routinely, at the end of the day, or randomly, when the plug is ripped from the wall socket by the user (see *denial*).

**slot:** 1. The long, thin receptacle on a credit card reader that beeps to indicate you have just spent another $1,000 on computer software. 2. An internal space in the computer designed by computer manufacturers to accept ever more hardware so they can continue to make money long after you have purchased your computer. Whether a credit card reader or internal space, the slot is the black hole of the computer world.

**software:** Those droopy forks and clocks that are always hanging around Salvador Dali paintings.

**spell checker:** A computor programmme witch cheks the speling of a righter. Yousful for riters who maybe gud riters but kant spel wurth a damm. Forchoonatly, the ritors of this buk are soo smart thay dont knead a spel chekker.

**shut down**

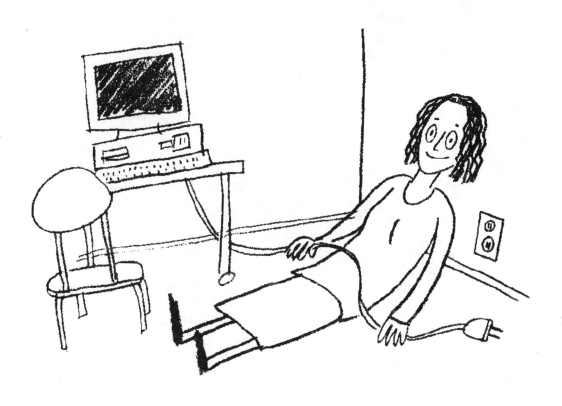

**syntax error**

**spreadsheet:**   A computer program that arranges and calculates finances and budgets. Before computers,
hardly anyone ever used spreadsheets. Not
surprisingly, after computers arrived everyone
needed spreadsheets to keep track of the large
amounts of money being spent every month.

**stack:**   Some people think a stack is a data storage
sequence. The rest of us, however, know that a
stack is a delivery mode for pancakes.

**superfloppy:**   A floppy disk used by a superhero. These
disks, when opened, contain such files as
"Anti-Kryptonite Control Panel" and "Bat
Cave Fast Find."

**syntax error:**   The closest your computer will ever come to
yelling at you "Hey! Dirtball! You messed it up
big-time!"

**SysRq:**   The key on IBM-style expanded keyboards just
to the right of F12. No one knows what it's for,
though rumor has it that pressing this key,
like stepping on a crack, will break your
mother's back.

**system error:**   A mistake made by the designers of system
software such that you cannot do what you really
want to do. The computer, however, would like
you to believe that the error is all your fault.

**system file:** A file used by the Macintosh to handle its internal operations. If the system file isn't in the system folder, the result can be a system crash, which, in turn, can cause system upset, also known as "Rolaids time."

***T*ab:** A drink that was popular in the seventies and sort of tasted like Coke, but not quite.

**technical writer:** A highly paid individual who writes in terminology that can be understood only by a highly paid consultant (see *computer publishing crime ring*).

**telecommunications:** A long word that generally means "sending a file to someone over a phone line." Despite popular belief, telecommunications has nothing to do with receiving letters, calls, or faxes from late "Kojak" star Telly Savalas.

**text:** Words in a word-processing document without all the cool stuff such as bold, italics, and outlining. Text is to a fully formatted document what the Republican convention is to a Lollapalooza concert.

**text-only:** A technique used to pass on a word-processing file to enemies such that they have to spend hours mindlessly putting underlining, italics, and bold print back in the document.

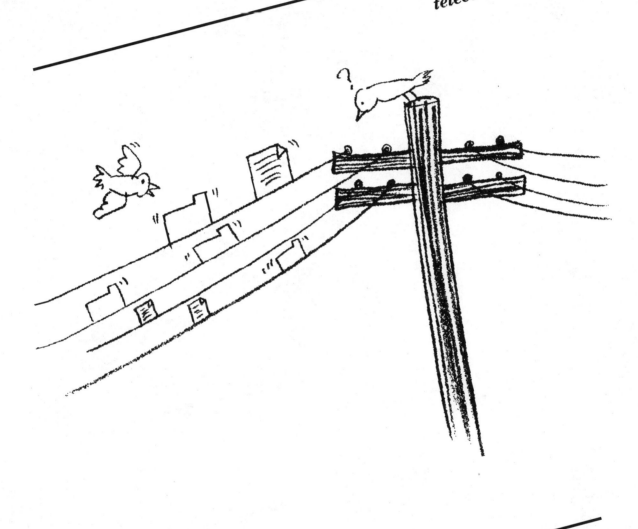

**trackball**

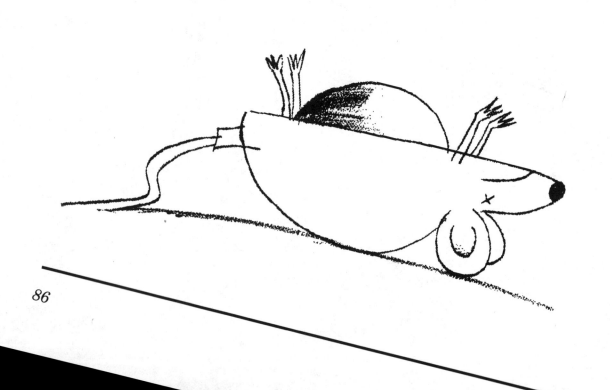

**trackball:** A mouse that has been turned upside down, much like a dead mouse. Because of this extra-ordinary design, a trackball costs at least one hundred dollars more than a normal mouse.

**trash:** An icon found in older, politically incorrect Macintosh computers. Newer models feature a "recycling bin," and in the future most computers will take this feature one step further by asking their users to reduce the number of waste files generated at their source. This will be done by working less or by not working at all.

**U***ndo:* A computer function that is always too late to use when you desperately want it, but can be used pretty much at any other time.

**upgrade:** An annual scheme to increase lagging sales and publicity in which software manufacturers improve their product by introducing new features that should have been part of the original system in the first place. This, of course, invariably introduces a new strain of robust, Raid-resistant bugs to the system, and slows the whole thing down.

**user-friendly:** Simply put, a lie propagated by the computer industry that suggests computers can be readily understood by anyone. If computers were really user-friendly, they'd tell you jokes, make you a cup of coffee in the morning, and cover for you when you want to leave the office at two o'clock on Fridays.

**utility:** Any little program or function that can be added to one's computer to make life with it a tiny bit more bearable (see *Jack Daniels*).

**Version:** The current model of a software package. The first version of any program is called Version 1.0. The people who buy Version 1.0 are called "guinea pigs," "hard-core computer nerds," or simply "suckers."

**video toaster:** An Amiga computer that makes your graphics all crispy and brown.

**virtual reality machines:** Highly advanced computers that simulate reality by interacting with many of the user's senses simultaneously. In the future, virtual reality machines will be employed primarily by programming nerds, who will no longer have to suffer the humiliation of trying to find a date.

**virus:** Any one of a number of computer ailments that can be prevented by practicing safe computing. However, abstinence from computer use is the only sure way to prevent viruses.

**voice mail:** 1. A computerized Byzantine maze through which callers must successfully route themselves so they may eventually be connected with a receptionist. 2. A means of using several minutes of long-distance telephone time and still having to call a person back.

*virus*

**Word**

**W**indows: A Microsoft program designed to make an IBM computer look and act like an Apple Macintosh. This is akin to dressing up your Uncle Norman in a torn flannel shirt and wig and having him lip-sync to Pearl Jam.

*wizzy-wig:* Pronunciation of the acronym WYSIWYG, which stands for "what you see is what you get" and refers to either the printout of a word-processing document or used car lots. The original term was coined by Flip Wilson, a comedian who used to dress in drag on his early seventies TV show and say, "What you see is what you get, honey!" From which we can only conclude that nerds' parents let them stay up late.

**Word:** In the beginning was Word, and Word was simple. A bunch of Words made a sentence. Now, Word is a complex labyrinth of commands, symbols, icons, and a lot of other things that aren't Words at all.

**About the Author:** Doug Mayer is the co-author of a number of humor books, including *The Cutting Edge, The Supreme Court: A Paper Doll Book*, and *Bill and Al's Excellent Adventure*. Doug owns, and has been known to use, an Apple computer.

**About the Illustrator:** While illustrating *The Slightly Skewed Computer Dictionary*, John Overmyer was hit by a truck and broke his humerus bone. He's better now, though a bit sore, and his sense of humor is intact. He lives in Philadelphia with his cat, Mimi, and produces editorial cartoons for newspapers across the country.